# This World of Selves

# This World
# of Selves

NEW
& SELECTED
POEMS

## Kevin Acers

Lampadina Press

Also by Kevin Acers:

*Time Machine: Prose Poems & Vignettes*
*Dead Mouse Poems*
*The Murder of Crows and Other Quirky Poems*
*Zippy Zappy: Diminutive Poetry*
*I am not a Dog and Other Poems*
*Simultaneous Everything*

ISBN:978-1-7357551-1-3

Printed in the United States of America

แด่

for
'Heep'
*doy rak*

ห

# CONTENTS

May pairs of children's eyes be born
that will count again
the ancient stars
and countless heads of grain
that will cover a transformed earth.

*Pablo Neruda*

# THE WORLD BENEATH OUR FEET

We spin while standing still,
for this is the nature
of the world. It spins, spins.

In our smallness it spreads before us
like an infinite plane.
This is an old illusion.

With our hands on our hips
we think we are giants
and have conquered something.

Meanwhile, we spin.
We spin and spin and spin.

## MOON

How strange
that the
moon

is inanimate,
incapable
of love.

## SHORT STORY

With the smell
of spilled gasoline
on my hands
I knew I couldn't
touch her, so
I let go of that wish
and relaxed.

As if I could have
touched her anyway.

*Down in the canyon the survivors were wailing in the overturned*
*car, but it was dark, the cliffs steep, so we drove on to the bar.*
— Jim Harrison


## PANIC IN THE WATER

Camus wrote of the decisive moment a person can face
when, strolling beside a river, one hears the cries of another
flailing in the water, who had fallen from the bridge.
Do we turn and keep walking, or do we jump into the water
to save that frightened stranger from drowning?

If being honest is a virtue, then I am virtuous in observing
that I have been both hero and coward at different times.

I think this is true of most of us: the one who takes the icy plunge
and the one who, with sinking heart, pretends not to hear the cries
and walks briskly away. One leads to unforeseeable entanglements,
the other to persuading oneself that nothing happened, only
to awaken abruptly on random nights for years, wondering.

## WORLDLY THINGS

The world is a many-eyed thing,
a many-testicled, many-minded,
many many-things thing.
Our feet are the world's feet,
our noses the planet's collective
olfactory glands, our tongues
the tongues of the earth.
Lizard tongues, rabbit tongues,
tortoise tongues, aardvark tongues,
your tongue and mine:
we give the world its sense of taste
and its weird articulations.
A spider has many eyes,
but nothing compared to the planet's.
The world sees through the eyes of squids,
penguins and toads, cocker spaniels and me.
Such ubiquitous sight!
The same applies to the world's many elbows,
its memories, its gills, its breath
and bones; its poems.  Its selves,
and all the other things.

## LUNCH AMONG THE CANNIBALS

Whom did you kill today? he queried.
I dropped onto the table the carcass of a fish.
Whose children shall we ravage? I countered,
and he tossed me one after the other
a spotted pear and two plump tomatoes.
We stopped talking then and gobbled down our spoils.

## ATOMIC SELVES

We knew the word 'atom' from school and of course
we knew — how well we knew — the word 'bomb.'

We did not know 'atomic' as an adjective for 'bomb,'
but abruptly and completely we became fast learners.

One hundred thousand of our selves instantly perished,
and if we consider subsequent generations, and future ones,

those missing selves multiply into millions at least.
So many selves, so many tandem blinks of eyelids,

so many occurrences of laughter, of respiration,
of clumsy stumbles, adulation, adorable smiles,

memories of playing with plastic figurines,
moments of rampage and shameless misdeeds,

misplaced judgments, well-placed feet balancing in boats,
yawns and whispers, weary baths and sudden sneezes,

palpitations of the heart when startled,
flashes of cruelty and whimsy and gnawing guilt,

well-ruminated plans,
stubborn principles,

so many aspects of so many selves, so many past selves
that are now anonymous and so many hypothetical ones

in the millions, in the billions, selves of the world
and would-be selves, so many selves that they may as well

themselves
be atoms.

## SEA CREATURES

The impossibly vast waters
of the sea
are perpetually pregnant.

Swollen bellies
of whales,
gelatinous eggs of squid.

O reproductive oceans!
You swirl with zeal,
a maelstrom of biology.

There is a constant motion
of procreation
hidden in the murk while

here on the world of dry ground
we also fill time and cities
with our blur of selves.

## THE TRUTH IS

I am not a hunter of ducks.
I am not a roller derby girl
with a fierce grimace
and an elbow held up high
poised to assault a competitor.
I am not a connoisseur of shellfish.
I am not a monkey
strapped into a capsule
atop a rocket marked CCCP
and launching into orbit
where I am doomed to die.
I am not a young boy hoeing
around melon vines to aerate the soil
and decapitate weeds.
I am not a beautiful meteorologist
named Cindy.
I am not an athlete spitting
brown saliva onto the field of play.
I am not a mechanic
whose beefy hands
are blackened with grease
from adjusting the gears
of a carnival ride.
I am not a large animal veterinarian.
I am not a disillusioned puppeteer.
I am not a funeral director
experiencing the effects
of generalized anxiety disorder.
I am not a Jesuit-in-training.
I am not a small town reporter
who drinks gin with lunch.
Most notably, I am not
a Tony Award nominee.

Maybe next year.

## LIFE LOVES LIFE TO DEATH

Moved by deep passion,
Life copulates with Life,
launching Life's fertile seed
into a uterine paradise.
"Ohhh, Life!" moans Life.

Life's swollen belly
shelters and incubates
Life's sprouting seed
until gestation is complete.
Life finally gives birth
to a baby, Death,
offspring of Life and Life.

"Life!" calls Life to Life
with exhaustion and joy.
"Look at our perfect child!
Death looks just like you!"

## HOLLOW SONGS

Missing dead friends
is the most hollow
of all the hollow songs

## THE WORLD HAS OTHER EYES
## WITH WHICH TO SEE
*For Peter*

The world has other eyes with which to see,
other tongues with which to speak,
and other working brains with which to speculate.

I find no solace in this notion as your own eyes dim,
your tongue becomes increasingly awkward,
your mind steadily less adept.

I cannot help but think that the world will note
with a shudder an abrupt downward shift
in its quirky imagination when you're gone,

its friendship with creative dissidents,
its sense of responsibility toward their poverty;
and its sentimental love for cats and coffee.

We must gird ourselves
 as we grapple, the Earth and I,
 hoping half-heartedly to compensate.

## LYNN

I think of you tonight
with whispering memories.
They twist like smoke rising in a wispy helix
from silent embers of long ago love,
a persistent, secretive wishing
that briefly defies grief.

## ON THE MORNING
## OF YOUR FUNERAL

I look into the rain,
feel an odd, comforting chill
and for a moment
imagine I am young,
you are alive, and
we are together.
Looking up, hand in hand,
we are unexpectedly
swallowed by a toad.
You laugh,
"It's dark in here."

# THE DREAM

*He runs the risk of being*
*just a shadow on the wall**
– Voice-over in a dream from which I've just
awakened


I am driving a car when two teenaged boys
deliberately ride their bicycles in front of me,
forcing me to brake abruptly. It is a passive-
aggressive power play to show who rules the
street – a street with a downhill slope. My
brakes fail, and the car races toward the boys
to the terror of us all. On the periphery, a
figure on the adjacent sidewalk comes into
view. It is Justin Timberlake, strolling
nonchalantly, hands in the pockets of his
black denim jacket. Silently observing the
scene, he looks on as I speed ever closer to the
boys, who out of desperation are trying to
pedal their bicycles backwards. The invisible
narrator reads his line.*

## WHERE WE STAND

We look so prim
stoically posing

in knee-high socks
where an ancient fish

once blindly swam
with its hungry snout

detecting amidst
the swirl of muck

a mad premonition
of our ankles.

## ANTIPHONY

Stones seek nothing in the grass.
Clouds float without pursuing infamy.
A tree does not ponder the future of its seeds.
Rain does not dread evaporation.
Birds do what they do without perceiving themselves.
Spiders kill neither for malice nor sport.
A hill does not contemplate its place in history.
Geysers, when they spew, are free
of a sense of accomplishment.
A central nervous system is central
only to transient units of life.

O human beings! Let us not overindulge
in identity. Let us be molecules
rather than fussy curators of self.
Let us invest in our capacity for perspective.
Let us allow our well-connected cells
to do to what they do without boasting
while we sit like a stone in the grass.
If we must seek something to honor our presence,
let it resemble justice, let it correct imbalance,
let it be sane and benign. Let it contribute hope
and characterize beauty; let it educate.
Let it be inseparate.

# MARGARET'S CURTAIN

"I am not that curtain," her student insisted.
I suppose I am saying you are, Margaret,
the quiet biologist, responded.

Everything is movement and particulate and wave
inhabiting space pretending at emptiness.
There is nothing solid about what seems most solid
and nothing inert about the most stationary thing.

It is not that you as we perceive you
are the curtain as we perceive it;
that supposes the curtain itself is a single thing –
and you – static within fixed margins.

You and I and the curtain are all a blur.
Separation among these so-called things
is an illusion, to paraphrase Einstein,
even if a stubborn one.

Don't get me started on now being then
and, like you and the curtain, tomorrow
being yesterday.

## *BUT I HEARD
ONLY TAMBOURINES

I found a lovely girl
from Philadelphia
who needed the world to be
a couple of steps behind.

We got on well together.
When it came time to leave
the world, I listened
for the sound of weeping...*

## I SEE SMALL FISH

I see small fish
swimming in her eyes,
fancy-tailed guppies,
one in each eye
hovering sideways
and waving their tails
like fabulous flags.
I am not even
slightly surprised.

## HOW TO BE A PENGUIN

I do not have any
reliable suggestions
other than these:
move to Antarctica,
grow slick feathers,
shrink to size,
squat on eggs,
earn the trust
of similar beings,
waddle in
a penguiny way,
subsist on little fishes,
and never engage
in flight.
With all of this, mind you,
it is likely you still
will never
become a penguin.
But if you can fool them,
you can probably
fool yourself.

## BONGO THE CLOWN

He performs at parties
for claps and laughter.

An unconventional clown,
he grasps at time and space.

He twists them into a lifetime
like balloons into poodles.

Soon he shall progress
to more inventive, abstract shapes.

Inflating with helium at last,
he will gently ascend.

Happily he'll rise,
sailing ever upward

far beyond the range
of giggles and applause

until at last he disappears
behind the moon.

Unable to sleep, at three a.m.
she hangs laundry on the clothesline
in the light of the harvest moon

## BENEATH A BOX

with the wind and the rain
and the heat, the snow
and the glare and the cover
of clouds in the night
and reflections of rays
of the sun from the moon,
with the noise and the light,
the silence of shadows
and stillness and whirl
of the mind of a man
looking up, looking in,
looking out, looking
drowsily nowhere.
He sleeps.

## DAVID'S FACE

His face resembles
the clouds of Jupiter.
See the swirls
of his cheekbones?
The giant storms
of his eyes?
Speculation abounds
as to what might dwell
beneath the visible
surface.
So much remains
a beautiful and
scientific mystery.

## BREAKFAST AT THE DINER

How do you want your eggs,
the waitress asked.
Transmogrified, I answered.
Scowling, she scribbled
on her pad without comment
and turned toward the kitchen.
I await the outcome hungrily
with eagerness and trepidation.
Suspense is a stimulant
stronger than coffee.

## THEY SAY THAT
## I WORRY TOO MUCH

A plethora of unborn
chickens wind up
in scrambled eggs.

The goddamn hens
don't care,
but *I* feel guilty.

## CURRENT RESIDENT

I am sending you
a poem through the mail
because there is an emotion
I hope you will experience

upon opening the mailbox,
flipping through bills
and envelopes addressed
to Current Resident,

and discovering a postcard
featuring on one side
a crayon drawing
of white clouds in a blue sky

and on the other side
a poem written by hand,
not composed in the service
of advertising anything.

It's a feeling you haven't had
in a while, is it not?

## ALCHEMY

A boy. A dog, a bicycle.

A shining Self emerges
from combining
basic elements with
just the right timing.

## BLOOD LOSES ITS SHAPE

Blood loses its shape
when it spills,
but otherwise it courses
through its natural habitat.
Holding the shape of the veins
that it fills, like water
holds the shape of a river,
it flows like traffic through
a seemingly infinite metropolis,
a city in constant motion
fueled by breath.

Once compromised, though,
once its barrier is broken
with a puncture or a slash,
once it leaves the tunnels
and gushes outside,
the uncontained blood
instantly loses its shape,
its sense of direction,
its function suddenly reduced
to nothing other than
feeding hungry flies.

## POST-MORTEM

Bones reduce to ashes,
wishes to silence,
worries to smoke.

Ashes ride the wind,
swirl in the water,
copulate with soil.

Entropy whispers:
*entity, old illusion* –
*disappear!*

Blue sky, white
clouds, shifting
wind, a pair
of eyes. This
is human
history.

## MISCELLANEOUS MUSES

A man has written a poem
for a man who has written poems
for any number of women
and only one man,
who has also written poems
for so, so many different people.
And also for snow, and donkeys.
For a leaf; for a kidney stone.

# FLOWER MAN

*News item, Dec. 11, 2020: Protest Follows Police Killing of Oklahoma City Man*

A disheveled middle-aged man, homeless and living with serious
mental illness, loiters in front of a pawn shop. He seems to be
arguing with himself. This leads the business owner to call
the police. He reports that the man is creating a disturbance.

An officer arrives at the scene. He approaches the man,
who is African American and openly carries a knife.
The officer talks to him, and regarding the knife perceives him
as hostile. He soon calls for back-up in case things get out of hand.

Two more officers arrive. They more or less encircle the man.
His name is Bennie, a familiar figure who hears voices in his head
and sells flowers on the streets. He is known in the neighborhood
as Flower Man, a friendly oddball who waves and smiles at passing
cars, holding up bouquets.

He feels trapped inside the circle of police. Increasingly agitated, he
doesn't drop the knife. He makes no threats but neither does
he surrender himself. He is afraid and confused.

Lessons repeatedly taught remain unlearned. This story unravels the
way so many before it have done. Bennie grows volatile. One of
the officers discharges pepper spray. This doesn't have the desired
effect — submission — and Bennie screams. Another officer shoots
a taser into Bennie's chest. This also fails to neutralize him. His
adrenaline goes wild. He panics. He bolts, wanting to run beyond
the police. Since they surround him, he has no choice but to run
directly toward them. As he does, he still clutches the knife
in his hand.

The officers react according to how they were trained. Their bullets
do what bullets do.  Shot in the back with multiple rounds, Bennie

exhales his last breath, face-down in the parking lot, onto the blood-wet cement.

Evening news reports blithely announce the policemen are on routine suspension. The people who knew Bennie are horrified.

Bennie no longer sells flowers, causes disturbances, sleeps outside, carries a knife, defies the police, hears disembodied voices, or bleeds.

In other words, this story has the usual ending.

## 'WALKING ON THE WALL OF SAINT-MALO, GAZING AT THE WINE-DARK SEA...'*

Seventeen years old, far from home. He stands alone and looks at the expansive sky, the ocean's horizon. Walking atop the famous town wall encircling Saint-Malo, he is moved by the simple convergence: himself, a stone wall, the night sky, the sea, behind him the old city and its streets. It is a pleasantly cool, increasingly purple night brightened by a quarter moon. Down below, his friends happily hop about in a throbbing discothèque aboard a dry-docked boat. He hurts, pining for a girl in America. Heartbreak releases itself in waves with a sea-like force. Gulping as his eyes unleash hot tears, he is at the same time becoming inspired. This is a special place, here on this wall. His weeping stops. A calmness comes and with it a melancholy gratitude. The urge to leap from atop the wall arises – an impulse not for self-harm but to be airborne. He wants to glide away. Instead he keeps walking with increasing tactile awareness of the stones beneath his sneakers. After a while he finds himself inventing a song.*

## THROUGH TEARS

My eighty-five-year-old father
at the bedside of his dying wife
leans forward and whispers
his final words to her, trembling.

## NEW YEAR RITES

The papal blessing is bestowed
with passionate compassion
from Saint Peter's Square

while, invisible to all
the faithful souls and skeptics
in this world of selves,

a platoon of manatees
use their bodies – all torso and tail –
to thrust themselves

through their fluid cathedral,
oblivious to contrivances
like calendars and gods.

## JANUARY FIRST

The calendar is a man-made thing
taken, I speculate,
more seriously by its inventors
than is justified,

an abacus of time
rendering into numbers
the movement of the sun
and its satellites as we age.

One could fairly say that
these segments of time
measured in grids and labeled
with names of obsolete deities

are as fictional as the myths
from which they derived.
Like two-faced Janus,
while a fascinating character,

the delineated squares are mythical,
collectively imagined.
That there is a moment when
a chapter of time Begins,

trussed against the backside
of the previous chapter's terminus,
is conventional hullabaloo.
There is no hour, week, or year,

no receding months accumulating
dusty glory nor forward-reaching ones
on a string strung with hopes
like cheery puffs of popcorn.

Is yesterday, only hours away
according to the mechanical
measures of the clock
and the calendar's tidy boxes,

something actually separate
from what we call today?
The calendar's printed pages
and sequences of numbers

counting our so-called days,
demarcations of temporal units
that have become our new gods
with prophesies of destiny,

are such a feeble mockery,
so laughably weak an exertion
of human impulse to control the wilds
when compared to the shifting

shadows on the visible moon,
the tilt of our worlds' angling
toward the sun, the tides; and yet
I do not pretend to be immune.

I, too, say "Happy New Year,"
even while maintaining that
two of those three words
are an illusion.

*There was a song they sang before I was*
*young*
– Robert Kelly


## WHAT WAS I BEFORE
## I WAS YOUNG?

The piano was still
until fingers
touched the keys.

    Are you saying I was a piano,
    or the silence of the keys?

Before you were young
the piano was silent
and even before that,
there wasn't a piano.

    Did the song come first
    or later?

The song?
The song is what you
make up along the way.

## PURPLE

Purple

is the
color
of a
bruise

and other
flowers.

## GALÁPAGOS

An anonymous insomniac
spends another night as usual —
quietly writhing,

tired face striped by slashes
of moonlight finding their way
through slats of the window blinds.

Meanwhile, stolid tortoises
in Galápagos, chewing in place,
boldly stare for centuries.

# PSYCHOLOGIES OF ATTACHMENT

In Buddhist psychology attachment cultivates misery
and suggests a practice of letting go
to reduce overidentification
with things both pleasing and abhorrent.

In family psychology attachment is a matter of balance,
patterns of connection either healthy or perverse,
determining the capacity for wellness
within oneself and between oneself and others.

In mechanical psychology attachment is achieved
through engineering, with various devices linked
with slots and nails and screws and buttons,
enabling components to work beyond themselves.

In biological psychology attachment is evolutionary
— leaves to stems, feathers to birds, tissue to bones;
whiskers to chins, leeches to ankles, toenails to toes —
its mutations are a function of survival.

In romantic psychology attachment can happen by choice
or through Fate's design, an emotional choreography,
the dancers losing balance which might be regained,
if only the lovers realized, through Buddhist psychology.

## I LOOK INTO A MIRROR
## AND I SEE THE FACE
## OF A DOG

It is the face of my childhood dog
the moment after
I stupidly smacked his snout
for no reason other than
the delusion that power
lends purpose to brutality.
It is the wounded face of dismay.

## THE HORSEFLY AND I

The horsefly takes me for a daily walk.
It wears a tiny collar, I wear a ring
and each is tied to the other
with a leash – this long silk string.
The horsefly leads me outside
and we go, often, to deposits
of fresh manure in the grass;
sometimes to the spot where a peach
rots beneath its mother tree;
or to a tail-whipped horse's rump.
Other times it rises, leading me aimlessly
as it meanders through the sky,
but not too high, just as high as its leash
is long, so that I can plod along
humming through my teeth
my horsefly's buzzing song.
While we try not to think or speak
of such things, we both understand
that I will likely outlive the fly.
I will wander alone then, wearing my ring,
dragging behind me my sad trail of string.

## SEASIDE RESORT

As we bob here in the sea,
my young love and I,
the surface waters are warm

but not far below
where we wriggle our toes
the water is cool

and a mile below that
the ocean is not
touristy at all.

# THE BOX

My friend and I, exchanging witticisms, were walking down the sidewalk when something caught my eye. It was a person squatting alone in an alleyway. I hesitated, and my friend kept walking. I waved him on; he ambled away with a shrug. The crouched figure a few yards away from where I stood held what looked like a shoe box. He gazed at it intently, then yanked off its lid, staring even more intently inside the empty box. Crestfallen, he then replaced the lid, stared again at the closed box and once more abruptly snatched the lid away with anticipation. With thrust-out chin and bulging eyes he stared inside the box before defeat again clouded his face. Undeterred, he kept repeating his efforts as I watched. I awkwardly approached him, clearing my throat, and asked what he was doing. He sized me up with benign indifference. He quietly responded, "Trying to catch it when it's still dark," as if this were obvious. "See," he explained. "It occurred to me that a closed box must be pitch black inside. I'd like to see that! But no matter how fast I pull off the lid, the darkness disappears before I see it." Then he mumbled, "Just not quick enough." He returned his attention fully to the box, ready to give it another try. I left him there, going on my way. Minutes later as I approached my apartment, I knew how I would be spending the rest of the night.

## AT THE SEA'S EDGE

She wished herself invisible,
believing it would bring relief
to obscure her place in this world.

Instead, she surprised herself –
running in frantic delight,
she chased her own glad footprints.

## THE FLEDGLING

No warmth from the autumn sun – it doesn't reach this tilt – only a subtle lightening of the grays. Fallen leaves mingle with withered decisions near my feet. They stir in the chill of a breeze and scoot away. Overhead, migratory birds come into view. I glance up just as a fledgling thought takes wing. It darts up to join the flock. Off they go in their wide-skied V.

## TONIGHT'S SKY IS KINETIC

Our bright, white moon
throws dramatic lighting
on the swiftly moving clouds
framed by silhouetted branches
of an old pecan tree resembling
a grandmother's arms opened
for a welcoming embrace.

## ODE TO GAZPACHO

I dreamed about
a small bowl
of gazpacho.
Feeling rushed,
I reluctantly
allowed myself
to pause for
one quick taste.
The flavors danced,
as they do.
Setting aside
my anxious haste,
I forgot my plans
and settled in
to savor every
spoonful.

## THE WORLD AT LARGE
## AND SMALL

The world doesn't know its name, but it blinks its several billion eyes at the sun (not in unison); stretches upward its countless trees (not in haste); and regurgitates itself in hot rivers of magma (not with a singular purpose). Meanwhile, its mosquitos copulate in flight. Humans too. Somehow this all makes a whole.

## AFTERMATH

If an asteroid or other careening body with similar heft
spins its way through space and crashes into the earth —

not apocalyptically to the point of demolishing the world
but enough to make a crater the size of Vermont,

enough to remind slumbering ancient hills
of the collision that did away with the dinosaurs,

enough to break off a big enough chunk to be caught
in our rattled orbit and gradually become a sphere —

will survivors' descendants dance in primitive awe,
beholding an eclipse of this second moon?

## BEAUTIFUL
## TABOO

When
a celibate priest
secretly writes
love poems
it is not
a prayer
or confession
but a secretion
of honesty,
the secreting gland
being the heart,
its chambers
including one
for regret,
one for joy,
and one
to harbor
hypothetical
passions.

Do birds fly
according to plans,
or are they always
making choices?

## MISSA LOOKS UP

The impulsive cat is running toward the old maple tree as if he expects to hurdle it. "You are not a cow," Missa admonishes him, "and this tree is not the moon." She scoops him up. The cat does not resist her interference. Missa walks slowly, cat in arms, tickling his belly. Once, twice, he spanks her with his tail. They both lift their eyes to the sky. Missa has long ago concluded that moments gazing skyward are not wasted. The cat, who Missa calls Buster, appears to be in agreement.

The maple tree's branches are catching a breeze; leaves quietly rustle. Far above, billowy white clouds scroll across the pale blue field. Two birds pass overhead, animated V's. Missa briefly enters a dimension of time suspended. All is still for a moment, including cognitions. Then the cat squirms, Missa levels her gaze, and she slips back into the world of selves.

## WHEN YOU UNEXPECTEDLY HEAR JOAN ARMATRADING'S *SHOW SOME EMOTION* AGAIN

*For Anne*

It is as if someone had made, all those years ago, a post-hypnotic suggestion:

Whenever you hear these songs, you shall return to the summer of 1986. Slightly wine-tipsy, you will dance as the sun goes down. You will sway in her arms in a modest house, its lights turned off. Your eyes will slide closed, open halfway, then close again. You will move to heartfelt rhythms as the plaintive vocals emotionally tattoo you. The swaying girl in your arms will again be wise at twenty-three, you will again be twenty-five and much less wise. The music will fill the room and you will float, the two of you, coaxed into a hush. You will relish this moment again, sweetly clinging to her and to the trite, futile hope that you will never reach the end of the song, that this sweetness will linger unhurried, unbetrayed by time.

Decades later you discover it somehow has.

# QUESTIONS FOR THE OUIJA BOARD

Where should we plant a flag
to designate the horizon?

What former continents conspired
to elope and beget the moon?

How much of this mountaintop will rise
someday as an island from the sea?

When will we stop forgetting
that our bodies are flying?

What is the absolute temperature
of silence?

Why do I imagine your eyes
would taste like apricots?

Who stares into mirrors and sees
exactly what they expect?

Does the naming of a new species
create debate among its population?

How important is the color
of blood to a dog who bleeds?

## SUMMER SOUNDS

Bitching little birds
tussle over seeds
scattered on the ground.

Eyes lazily blinking,
the drowsing dog suddenly
snaps its jaws at a fly.

We barely notice
the air conditioner's
mechanical hum.

Halving a hefty melon,
the long knife hits the cutting board
like a guillotine.

Hidden cicadas
collectively obliterate
the afternoon's quiet.

A quintessentially metallic
scraping and pop –
aluminum cans open with a hiss.

Two chatting neighbors
share beer on the porch
and laugh.

After the sun goes down,
randy cats perform
their raunchy opera.

Like a battering ram,
thunder splits the night:
an unexpected summer storm.

I imagine watching you sleep,
touching you with nothing but breath.

Even this whisper is a dream.

## DOMINO EFFECT

Accounts of the man who swallowed himself whole are circulating widely. Restlessness stirs in the hearts of those who outwardly judge him. They mutter *what a fool*, masking with derision painful doubts about their own fates.

If it could happen to him, their inner voices quiver, what is to keep me from gulping myself down? What triggered his self-ingestion? Was it gluttony? Madness? An awkward accident? Was he chewing on his lip and tripped on an uneven sidewalk? Or was it something more sinister — a saboteur, perhaps? Did someone push him hard from behind just as he was yawning like a hippopotamus?

There may be no answers for questions like these.

If you pay close attention,
everything you stare at
is a mirror.

## A SOFT SWEET PAIN

I dreamed I sat with my family at the table
where we'd shared so many meals.

My late mother's body was slumped in one of the chairs.
I stared at her pale dead face.

"I miss you," I confessed. At these simple words
her pale cheeks flushed with color.

Her eyes opened, gazing squarely into mine.
She smiled and quietly stated: "Of course you do."

I awakened, much like my mother in the dream,
roused by a soft, sweet pain.

# SURVIVORS OF THE FLOOD

While 40 days and nights of rain
created quite the flood,
transforming the globe into
a water ball the color of mud,
it wasn't as complete a deluge
as Noah's worried prophesy
had led him to believe.
Scattered around the world's
submerged land masses
the topmost branches
of the oldest trees pierced
the water's surface, craggy fingers
dripping in the rain-drenched air.
On some of these branches
perched emaciated birds
suffering in the storm, weird little
claws clasping the thin branches
that poked up through
the waters.
Soaked and miserable,
feathers ruffled backwards
by wind and rain,
heads pivoting to the various
angles their necks afforded,
the birds silently sat it through.
Those that starved toppled
each with a tiny splash
into the deepening sea.
Those that managed to persevere
did not do so happily.
When, on day forty-one,
the sun emerged and the clouds
dissipated, sky clearing,
flood just starting to recede,

the emaciated birds were rankled.
They searched for human faces
gazing upward in giddy faith
upon which to descend
in vengeful swoops,
pecking those horrid eyeballs
with all the feeble might
their beaks could muster.
Humanity had screwed
things up again.

IF I COULD WRITE
IN JAPANESE, I WOULD
PAINT THESE WORDS
WITH DELICATE
STROKES ON THE CUP
FROM WHICH
I DRINK MY TEA

Your face
My face

Plenty of staring
while pretending
not to be staring –

an ordinary day

What has become of the girl I saw
thirty years ago sitting on the stairs
with her head in her hands, motionless
except for her long cigarette's
rising thread of smoke?

# THE HUMAN BEING

Waiting to order nachos,
I sit alone surrounded
by Caucasians.

I feel like some kind
of social daredevil.
My life is astounding.

Exhilarated, I quietly cling
to my gizmo with its
touch-screen keyboard.

My server tells me her name is Zoe.
I am tempted to ask whether
that is short for Zoology.

She seems a sweet child,
so I refrain from
such awkward semi-cleverness.

After placing my order I wonder
whether I am only pretending
to be a human being out of

Caucasian peer pressure,
hypervigilance,
or some practical nicety.

Here and in this moment
I suspect that Zoe alone
is truly human.

The rest
of us,
pretenders.

Now that I recognize her
authenticity I decide I shall
leave her a sizable gratuity.

This may distract her from
questions as to whether
I am of an unfamiliar species.

Plus, who knows,
perhaps she'll regard me
as a kind old uncle.

Of course she will soon
forget me, my nachos,
and my generous tip.

This is how it should be.
I will forget her as well,
along with my splendid nachos.

I sense with confidence
that Zoe will endure
as a singular human being.

This warms my other-than-
human heart. For now, at least.
And now is forever enough.

A child's mouth opens
and the rain falls in.

## NOTES FROM A HOT TUB

I stretch tired limbs into the churning water and look at the sky. Serious clouds fly past the moon. They are on the move, as if mobilizing in response to an incursion. The edges of the clouds are caught in silhouette against the moon standing guard with its bright white light. Occasionally the clouds drift apart, leaving the lunar sentry to shine alone in a brief black field of self-importance. I shift attention to my more immediate airspace as a firefly wanders near. It drunkenly staggers closer, within arm's reach, irregularly blinking as it roams back into the night. "If that was an enemy scout sent to gather intelligence," I pledge to the stoic moon, "I swear it found none here."

## QUESTIONS MY UNCLE TOLD ME HE PONDERS
## WHILE BREATHING THROUGH THE PAIN

If a cormorant had a human-like mouth, would it eat with
a fork or a spoon?

In a language with no written vowels, how would one
spell out a scream?

Do alpine goats assume yodelers are injured?

Does the world have a sense of right-side up
or upside down?

What does a newborn baby miss the most?

What could calm a rodent's racing heart?

To what extent am I residue versus something always new?

Why do people both fear and long for the company of
strangers?

Are houseplants always victims of abduction?

How many questions could there be to all the answers?

## ICICLE FINGERS

What species of death is this,
its icicle fingers pointing down
into the small dark hole
that once held a post
from the frame of a swing
in my childhood garden?

"You are a study
in micro- and
macrobiology,"

she said
into a mirror
as if practicing.

## THE WIDOWER'S DIET

The widower eats nothing
but raisins, wind, and snow,
and when there is no snow
radiation from the sun,
the occasional snack of gravel
coated in cocoa (memories
tasting like joy but breaking teeth),
and more rarely a handful of sugar
followed by a handful of salt.
These meals are taken while
heavily breathing, walking
with a long wooden stick
through the woods on a mountain –
looking for a new kind of happiness.

## SHE

She cleaned the house so obsessively that finally there was nothing more to sanitize, so she went into the garden with the vacuum attached to a long extension cord and sucked up all the dirt.

○

She searched her hardened heart and discovered a strange, unexpected softness engaged in movement — a sloshing and the swinging open and slamming shut of doors.

○

She would squint at herself in the mirror when she was fifteen, trying to see what her face would look like when she was fifty (which was as ancient as she could fathom). She could not really imagine herself with wrinkles or a fuller, slightly sagging face. Now fifty, she stares at herself in the mirror with eyes wide open. She sees nothing of herself at fifteen.

○

She lay flat in the grass, face warmed by the early May sunshine — a brief respite of Spring before summer's blistering heat. An invisible insect faintly buzzed nearby. Clouds posed, suspended in three dimensions in the distance, set off by the sky's blue backdrop. She closed her eyes and let her busy mind wander, first to loud reminders, then receding into a muffled mumbling as if behind a wall.

The unique joy
of ululating women
leaps across the meadows
like a doe.

## EARLY DECEMBER

Is there truly, in the end, such
a thing as a brown sweater?
Worn much less by a figure in
a round hat? This person
beneath the hat whistles until
realizing it is the melody from
an old song that he or she
despises. The sick wind blows
with a biting cold that feels
unjust.

## TAKING OUT THE TRASH ON A WINTER NIGHT

The snow is coming down in tiny specks from unseen heights.
It looks like a massive, disoriented swarm of flying insects.
The night is silent but its busy winds set these impossibly
light-weight ice-flakes swirling, rising, swooping,
dancing far above the ground as if resistant to gravity
for a long moment, while their predecessors rest
on the ground dormant, shiny like glitter reflecting spits of light,
cheering on their brethren who haven't yet landed.
They are as countless as all of nature's other countless things,
crystals woven into frozen fabric covering the grass,
those aloft filling the vast atmosphere all the way down
to my feet. It is all perfectly ordinary.  Perfectly.

## ICE FISHING

The Man in the moon sits
on an upside-down bucket,
holding a fishing pole whose line
drops into the small circle of a crater
cut into the ice at his feet
even though everyone knows
that up in space the fish don't bite.

Down below it's rush hour
on a cold morning.
A Kiowa named Joe, vaguely drunk,
sits on a five-gallon bucket
at a busy intersection,
manhole cover at his feet.
He holds a cardboard sign whose words
face the traffic ("Anything Helps"),
even though everyone knows
car windows in this town
don't open on winter mornings
to hand dollars to red-eyed Kiowa
staring into space.

Joe looks up while he tosses back
the last drops from his bottle
wrapped in a paper sack.
He sees the pale full moon
still high in the daytime sky.
The Man sees Joe too and waves,
calling down, "Nice bucket."
Looking down at his sign, Joe lets it fall
beside the manhole thinking,
What's the use. I might as well be
up on the moon.  Might as well be
ice fishing in space.

Final thoughts of a dying brain
whose eyes look out the window:

*I'm going to be outlived*
*by melting snow.*

*Algebra, a language spoken on the moon.*
Barbara Kingsolver, *The Lacuna*


## INTERPRETING ALGEBRA

O lone parenthesis!
Your message is indecipherable,
your dipthong incomplete.
Pondering your puzzle, I gaze past you
at the dust between your presence
and the horizon, above which floats
the semi-shadowed world.
Are you so avant-garde
as to stand alone without meaning,
or are you asserting yourself
as something symbolic? A single consanant,
the start of a word that sticks in the throat?
Are you hinting that incompleteness
is your complete condition — or ours,
as we haplessly attempt negotiations
between our dialects?
Are you expressing the futility
of language to encapsulate
the depths and breadths of perception?
Or is it, possibly, that perception
is itself as futile as a single parenthesis
proposed as an equation?
It is as if an oral historian
has opened her mouth to sing
and swallowed her tongue.

(

# FINAL ARRANGEMENTS
*With apologies to Mrs. Gallagher*

The funeral home director
informed me that cremated remains
are less like ashes and more like kitty litter.
I am not sure what to do with this information.
I can tell you that it disappoints me,
but I cannot explain why. He shows me our receptacle
options. I do not want an urn, that much is clear;
what an awkward thing to keep on a shelf.
I choose to go with a cardboard box, thinking
if nothing else it will motivate its guardian
to dispose of the thing and its contents
fairly soon. Then I remember going to see
my friend Tom in his small, not-so-tidy house.
Accepting his invitation to take a seat
required making room for my buttocks on his sofa
covered with nondescript stuff strewn about.
I nudged a cardboard box over to the side.
This alarmed normally mild-mannered Tom.
He leapt up with arms outstretched
as if to receive a well-defended basketball.
"Oh!" was all he could say. Then, "Mother."
I had attended her funeral a few months before.
I handed her condensed body in its plain white box
to Tom with a most peculiar feeling.
Now, here I was sitting with the pleasant
funeral planner, thinking of that moment with Tom.
That his mother's remains looked like kitty litter,
as I'd just learned my own would, unsettled me.
I take some comfort in knowing that my wife,
assuming she is the one who will end up with my box,
would never let it clutter up the house.
Perhaps she will use it for what it resembles
and give it to the cat.

## VASECTOMY

The stern-looking physician and his comely assistant are staring with awkward intensity at my scrotum. I am unaccustomed to this kind of attention. I, however, seem to have disappeared except for that carefully shaved body part. As the urologist gingerly inventories its interior ropes and pulleys, I silently praise modern science for local anesthesia. The doctors slice their tiny targets. They mumble together while cauterizing the freshly severed vas deferens, wispy threads of smoke rising as if from a miniature train. "Wooooooo, woooooooooooo!" I quietly sing. I don't care what they think. I provide my own sound effects.

## THE LIFE CYCLE
## OF WATER

Raindrops
do not care about
their numbers

or strive
to break
records

even
when
they do;

their egos
are small
and kinetic,

their
accomplishments
transformative,

their natures
ephemeral and
ignorant,

much like
being
alive.

## WHEN THE BELLS RING

When the bells of her breasts ring
it sometimes is as if I am deaf
or am watching a silent film.
I see the bells swing with no sound,
sweet echoes left to my imagining.

Other times I clearly hear the tones
when their ringers strike the bells.
It is not a jingle-jangle
like from the small round bells
on Native dancers' ankles.

It is not the irregular harmonies
a breeze can release from a set
of metal wind chimes made
from tubes of varying length.

It is not the somber tone of iron bells
the size of cows suspended outside
a Zen temple in the heart of Japan
and struck with swinging logs.

When the bells of her breasts ring
it is opera. They sing in every language
but mine, and this is good because
I would not want to be
distracted by the lyrics.

I want to hear the music.

## READING A POEM*
*Arthur Sze's poem "Strawberries in Wooden Bowls"*

Reading a poem about bowls of fruit, my mind keeps veering into memories. I stop rereading the poem and attend to my thoughts. Thoughts of a friend whose life ended a dozen years ago. The letters we'd exchanged. Helping him, in a death row cell, plan his funeral. The knowledge of what led him there. The bewildering futility of trying to reconcile this kind man with that violent act. Testifying at his final hearing watched by a woman who once loved him and whose mother he'd killed. Cringing at her raw and complicated pain while we endured once again an accounting of the brutal details. His last words to me an hour before the execution. Standing outside the prison on that cold January night with his mother, his sister, his ten-year-old daughter around whose shoulders I wrapped a blanket as he was quietly killed inside. What does any of this have to do with these lines? – "The strawberries in the wooden bowls / are half-covered with curdled milk."

# WHITE NOISE

Biscuits on a plate.
Two floor lamps.
A baseball bat.
Sometimes all there is
to a play are the props.
An unopened tube
of lotion prescribed
to soften scar tissue.
A white noise device
generating static.
A square table
with one of its legs
shorter than the others
propped on a book.
A sweater on a peg.

## MIGRATION

I find that I am not a semi-invisible,
semi-inanimate mute with a blunted affect,
jostling from the vibrations of a city bus
among equally translucent strangers.

I am, to my surprise, a darting flash of red
among an unexpected flock of parakeets
wheeling through the airspace
just above these city streets.

## A COLONY OF SELVES

A self-contained organism
when viewed through a microscope
is revealed to be a set of many subsets,
the circle of light shining
on a constant swirling swarm
of many moving parts, each of which
could have its own biography.

Through what lens do we gaze
when we lift our faces from the microscope
and perceive an individual self
standing across the room?
Is it truly a self — or is its set a subset, too?
What is the distinction between
perceiver and perceived?
Who is looking through the lens?
Is the single self a self or a colony of selves?

The world's body language, if we could read it,
offers a cryptic answer: "who" is illusory.

## COMMUTER

The mud that
splattered
this side of the bus
rides free all day

## SOCIAL WORKER AS WITNESS

I am working separately with two homeless men, both proudly Black and each having strengths of character and interesting quirks. One is just beginning to taste adulthood, the other acerbically startled to see cancer depleting what is left of his.

The cocky 24-year-old sees himself at the beginning of things. His dramatic, naïve certainty of future wealth contrasts to the seventy-nine-year-old toothless man filled with metastasis. The old man sleeps in the burned-out shell of his childhood home. The charred rafters and surrounding rubble are a trite metaphor as mortality's blaze spreads inside him, a crawling fire consuming its fuel.

I see the young man in the old. He is wickedly lively with mischief. Likewise, a patriarch stares from the younger man's depths as he enters a cavern into which he will expand. I will work with them both, but they'll never meet. In this context I ponder the next fifty days. The next fifty years.

## THE JETSONS

As a small boy
never did I imagine
an advertisement
for underwear
on a telephone
with a digital screen
boasting the slogan,
"Let the boys
breathe!"
Flying cars –
*that* I imagined.

## PRAJAPATI

Like Prajapati,
the anciently imagined
personification
of All,

each of us
is known by a name,
while our true name
will always be *Who?*

# SHADOWS OF SELVES

Shadows, sensing incompleteness,
search for the Selves that cast them.
In this process many hours pass.

The sun rises higher overhead.
The blind shadows grow desperate,
shrinking till at last they disappear.

Without their shadows
the Selves, who were there all along,
suddenly feel invisible.

# SHIRLEY AND THE DEVIL

A lean white dog,
friendly and charming,
came with the house
we rented. The house was
one of a few tucked away
among the landlord's groves
of mango trees. He told us
the dog had wandered
one day onto the acreage
and made herself at home.
White Dog, as he'd named her,
was a cheerful dog.
Each morning and evening
the landlord fed White Dog
leftovers he placed
in a makeshift bowl
fashioned from a blown-out tire.
I decided White Dog needed
a proper name. I called her Shirley.
When I slipped into baby-talk,
which would often
automatically occur,
I'd call her Shirley-girlie.
She was friendly and responsive.
One day after work I bicycled
onto the property
to discover Shirley in a state
of intense agitation. Her short
white fur bristled on her spine.
Her demeanor was deadly serious;
her attention fierce and focused
on the ground. Lips receded,
she barked and growled,

lunging erratically then jumping
back with primordial reactions.
Then I saw the cause for her anguish:
a large snake's abandoned, scaly skin.
I tried to calm Shirley with baby-talk.
She didn't seem to know I was there,
so intent was her focus on the danger.
The landlord approached,
sensing that I was about to intervene.
"Better not," he said. Wise words.
Another stray dog or two
had heard the commotion and
came to see what the fuss was about.
Soon they, too, were in a frenzy.
I wondered if they'd ever encountered
the inhabited skin of a snake,
but I realized it didn't matter.
That this translucent skin
was limp in the dirt and empty of life
did not diminish, for the dogs,
the situation's urgency.
I walked my bike around
the ongoing drama and
made my way to the house.
While moved by her boldness,
I felt sorry for Shirley-girlie, wishing
I could ease her alarm. For days
her genetic code remained on high alert.

# THEY COME AT NIGHT

Memories creep beneath your window, rustling the bushes. They worry you awake as you imagine a prowler or, trying not to panic, a skunk. Memories from which you recoil with a sharp gasp like from the startling pain of stubbing a toe in the dark. Silent memories that sail kite-like across a moonlit sky, trailing a broken string. Memories that disorient like a Wolf Man movie dubbed in an unknown language. Memories that occur microscopically like germs in a cut. Memories that haunt like the omens that trouble superstitious sailors at sea. Memories both awkward and beautiful like a small girl playing a bassoon. Protective memories that pull you close while you sleep, whose steady breath you can feel on your cheeks. Finally, memories that kiss, in whose waters you easily drown as you swim deeper and deeper to seek the source of the water's warmth. Reaching the bottom in joyful blindness you embrace the mud. Eyes still closed, mouth open and yearning, you feel in the gulping darkness for more, more, more memories that kiss.

# A HORSE'S TONGUE

Tell me with your equine eyes
leering at me sideways,

wary and warning,
about the salt lick

your flattened paintbrush
of a tongue shellacks

with saliva
again and again,

coat after coat,
lapping irresistibly —

consuming, sculpting,
creating and recreating.

## NOT FROM
## CONCENTRATE

This juice pressed
from apples
tastes so much like apples
that apples don't taste
like apples anymore.

## EVEN BIRDS

Even birds at the end
of a long, arduous day
sleep and relive in dreams
their numerous songs
retelling the same stories
over and over, persuading
themselves of significance.

# GOVERNMENT OF THE GODS

Primordial chaos created profane culture,
a fragile achievement
of disorder and disintegration.
Priests recite the Enuma Elish.
The epic poem clothed in idiom
a formless, watery waste
alien to the gods or human beings —
divine stuff, the swampy wasteland,
the frail works of men:
a sloppy mess where everything
lacks identity.

extrapolated from Karen Armstrong's *The History of God*, p. 7:

order out of primordial chaos, when they had created the world. The eleven sacred days of the Festival thus projected the participants outside profane time into the sacred and eternal world of the gods by means of ritual gestures. A scapegoat was killed to cancel the old, dying year; the public humiliation of the king and the enthronement of a carnival king in his place reproduced the original chaos; a mock battle reenacted the struggle of the gods against the forces of destruction.

These symbolic actions thus had a sacramental value; they enabled the people of Babylon to immerse themselves in the sacred power or *mana* on which their own great civilization depended. Culture was felt to be a fragile achievement, which could always fall prey to the forces of disorder and disintegration. On the afternoon of the fourth day of the Festival priests and choristers filed into the Holy of Holies to recite the *Enuma Elish*, the epic poem which celebrated the victory of the gods over chaos. The story was not a factual account of the physical origins of life upon earth, but was a deliberately symbolic attempt to suggest a great mystery and to release its sacred power. A literal account of creation was impossible, since nobody had been present at these unimaginable events: myth and symbol were thus the only suitable way of describing them. A brief look at the *Enuma Elish* gives us some insight into the spirituality which gave birth to our own Creator God centuries later. Even though the biblical and Koranic account of creation would ultimately take a very different form, these strange myths never entirely disappeared, but would reenter the history of God at a much later date, clothed in a monotheistic idiom.

The story begins with the creation of the gods themselves—a theme which, as we shall see, would be very important in Jewish and Muslim mysticism. In the beginning, said the *Enuma Elish*, the gods emerged two by two from a formless, watery waste—a substance which was itself divine. In Babylonian myth—as later in the Bible—there was no creation out of nothing, an idea that was alien to the ancient world. Before either the gods or human beings existed, this sacred raw material had existed from all eternity. When the Babylonians tried to imagine this primordial divine stuff, they thought that it must have been similar to the swampy wasteland of Mesopotamia, where floods constantly threatened to wipe out the frail works of men. In the *Enuma Elish*, chaos is not a fiery, seething mass, therefore, but a sloppy mess where everything lacks boundary

*So sue me*
*God said*
*to the disgruntled priest,*
*I never said*
*the matter-world would satisfy.*
— Robert Kelly

## THE TASTE OF APRICOTS

The world of matter
is satisfying enough:
its greens and blues,
its redwoods and wild roses,
its temperature swings;

its sulphur-scented springs
steaming among regurgitated mountains,
its levitating clouds of outlandish size,
its shadow periodically cast upon the moon;

its configurations of molecules
that connect throughout this physical self
among aches, pains, sorrows, laughter,
hypotheses, passions, secretions,
and various phenomena coalescing
into an identity which complex forces
mold from breath and mud.

Together these material things
are as close to spirit
as one would dare to hope.
The taste of apricots
is sacrament enough.

# EXISTENTIAL SOUP

Sentient aspects of the organism conjure a sense of self, deriving identity from a soup attended by too many cooks in the kitchen.

In the bottom of the pot squat chunks of the bones of a beast, while genes and chromosomes scurry like nanobots to engineer the broth among bits tossed in (cilantro, basil, parsley, bay leaves, rock-salt, a glass eye, some great grandparents' residual childhood trauma...). The unseen chefs share a consensus: "just throw it all in." Ingredients go into the pot in perpetuity, blending into an ever-changing concoction: hints of neurosis, shame, physical idiosyncrasies, fear, pride, moral leanings, musical preferences, political sensibilities, sentimental proclivities, allergies, compassion, gastric urges, desire, awe, and other culinary secrets.

The sentient components are stirred up, aside from fleeting moments of deceptive calm. Soon enough the recurrent questions arise: am I the soup or am I the pot in which it simmers, or the whole shebang? What must be protected, for what inadequacies should I attempt to overcompensate, what should be enjoyed and who will enjoy it and how will I know and when can I retire? (How sublime to imagine lazily steaming in a fancy tureen!) Meanwhile, who are all these people in the kitchen?

Then the weird, shameful questions: what is this impulse to consume myself, swallow by swallow? Maybe just a taste or two...what will it lead to? How long would it take before I am gone? If I don't eat me, who will? I wonder...I hope...am I delicious?

## BEAUTY PAGEANT

I declare each wave as it gracefully reaches the shore
where I sit on the warm wet sand

to be the most beautiful wave to walk across this stage.
Each in succession briefly wears the crown.

# ANTELOPE VALLEY

*'Two lizards doing push-ups in the sun...'*
— Coreen Knox

She admires desert reptiles for their daily calisthenics,
the countless repetitions of their anaerobic blinks.

To warm up they color-match themselves
to the hues of sun-baked rocks in the pale dry dirt.

With elbows bent they flex their well-toned tongues.
Their biceps are modest, but their stamina is impressive.

Unmotivated to achieve a muscular abdomen, they never preen.
They are moved by instincts more basic than vanity.

They demonstrate indifference to the gaze of this woman
who squats nearby to admire their physiques.

Immune to her pheromones,
their cold blood fails to stir.

Their stoic strength inspires her to stand finally,
smiling, and lift the weightless sky.

## TOY TRUCK

I was generally not a violent child
nor am I a violent man.
This disclaimer aside, I recall the brutal joy
that came from repeatedly throwing
against the pavement a yellow Tonka Truck.

I smashed it onto our driveway
with exuberant passion.
It was made of sturdy metal,
but I managed to inflict significant damage.
Scrawny and timid, I shied away from sports,
but Truck versus Concrete was a contest
I could appreciate.

My father came upon me just as I made
another gleeful, downward throw.
He had given me the truck as a present.

He angrily yanked me away from
my destructive entertainment demanding,
"Why would you do such a thing!"
It was a legitimate question
for which I had no answer.

As instructed, I went to my room
where I quietly sat wondering
whether I might one day die in Vietnam.

## IMAGINE YOURSELF

The instructions came in the mail. They were typed on an index card using a manual typewriter. The alignment of the letters was slightly askew, the ink gray, as if hammered from a well-used ribbon.

"Imagine yourself the roofer of a bungalow," the directive instructed. "Its owner is far away. Wherever he is, he is skipping outdoors. He is wearing plum-colored lipstick. He is mentally reliving past agonies, past moments of joy, childhood dreams. You, meanwhile, are here to repair the roof. You stand on a ladder brandishing a nail-gun. Now, look up! Search the sky, feel yourself being inexplicably moved, euphoric, inspired. Climb onto the roof."

It was not the sort of letter I often receive. Flinging wide the door I strode outside. I excitedly exclaimed, "I shall comply!"

## AND IN THIS MOMENT

The vast trouble world
is lit with anonymous flickers
of madness and grace.

Through tears of grief
an insomniac
is staring at the moon.

Crazed squirrels race in pairs,
running in spontaneous spirals
up trunks of wide-girthed trees.

A silent hawk coasting on thermals
glides without beating its wings
as if holding its breath.

A very serious dog
digs into the snow
with frantic passion.

And in this moment
on several
different continents

humans and their housecats
are mewing at each other
in their kitchens.

## MY WIFE IN THE GARDEN

She tilts her face upward, eyes gently closed
as she enjoys the sensations of Spring.
Three white geese are flying overhead.
These swan-like creatures feel shame
when, glancing down, they see her upturned face
and the ease of its beauty.
They fold their wings to cover their eyes
and drop from the sky, each with a similar thud.

## I DREAMED LAST NIGHT

I dreamed last night of a large brown owl. Solemn and haughty, it perched on a moonlit branch. Then I spotted another nearby. The longer I peered into the branches, the more owls I came to see. Golden-eyed and somber, their heads pivoted with bold, grave faces fixed on mine.

I soon made out the gleaming sheen of peacocks, too, startling-blue peacocks scattered in the heights of the trees, snoozing like cats. The stern owls stood guard, vigilant, poised for swooping flight.

Owls and peacocks! I stared amazed, standing barefoot in the ivy-covered grass. Leaning into the night I pointed, "Look! Look!" as if to exclaim, "Ordinary life — even *our* ordinary life — is spectacular!"

## NOTES

This book includes dozens of poems that have never before been published, along with revised versions of many that appear in the poet's previous collections: *Time Machine, Dead Mouse Poems, I am Not a Dog, The Murder of Crows and Other Quirky Poems, Zippy Zappy,* and *Simultaneous Everything.* Several of the poems have appeared in slightly different form in literary journals. The poem "Government of the Gods" consists of words and phrases drawn from a single page of *The History of God* by Karen Armstrong, Ballantine Books (1993).

## ABOUT THE POET

Kevin Acers has worked as an educator, a human rights activist, a Peace Corps volunteer, and a social worker. He holds master's degrees in TESOL (Teaching English to Speakers of Other Languages) and Social Work. His writings have appeared in a number of publications. This is his seventh book. Two previous poetry collections have been selected as finalists for the Oklahoma Book Award, and he has been a Pushcart Prize nominee. He lives in Oklahoma City with his wife, their cat, and a potted plant named Fronds Kafka.

www.ingramcontent.com/pod-product-compliance
Lightning Source LLC
Chambersburg PA
CBHW021117130626
46554CB00002B/737